PUERTO RICO
in Pictures

Linda Tagliaferro

Lerner Publications Company

Contents

Website address: www.lernerbooks.com

Lerner Publications Company
A division of Lerner Publishing Group
241 First Avenue North
Minneapolis, MN 55401 U.S.A.

web enhanced @ www.vgsbooks.com

THE ECONOMY   56

► Operation Bootstrap. Manufacturing. Service
Industries. Transportation. Agriculture and
Fishing. Mining, Forestry, and Construction.
The Future.

FOR MORE INFORMATION

Library of Congress Cataloging-in-Publication Data

Tagliaferro, Linda.
     Puerto Rico in pictures / by Linda Tagliaferro. — Rev. and expanded
        p.   cm. — (Visual geography series)
     Includes bibliographical references and index.
     ISBN: 0-8225-0936-9 (lib. bdg. : alk. paper) 27.93j
        1. Puerto Rico—Juvenile literature. 2. Puerto Rico—Pictorial works—Juvenile literature. I. Title.
II. Visual geography series (Minneapolis, Minn.)
     F1958.3.T34 2004
     972.95—dc21   2003000394

                                              j 972.95
                                                TAG

Manufactured in the United States of America
1 2 3 4 5 6 - JR - 09 08 07 06 05 04

INTRODUCTION

The lush, beautiful island of Puerto Rico is bounded by the Atlantic Ocean to the north and the Caribbean Sea to the south. Although Puerto Rico is small, its population of more than 3.8 million makes it one of the most crowded places in the world.

Neither a state nor an independent country, the island has been a possession of the United States since 1898. Its unique status is that of a commonwealth, or "free associated state." This status means Puerto Rico's residents can make decisions about local matters on the island, but they cannot vote for the president of the United States. Puerto Ricans do not pay U.S. federal income tax, but they can serve in the U.S. armed forces. They may live in the United States without applying for visas, as foreign nationals are required to do.

The first inhabitants of the island were peaceful peoples who lived off the land. Known as the Archaics, they dwelled in caves and made simple tools from stones and shells. By 1493, during the second voyage of Christopher Columbus, the Taíno Indians were living on the island.

The Spaniards established a permanent settlement in 1508, and in 1510, Juan Ponce de León became the island's first governor. Puerto Rico remained a Spanish colony for about four hundred years. The Spaniards virtually enslaved the Taínos, and eventually the island's native inhabitants died out.

By the 1800s, many Puerto Ricans wanted independence. After a series of rebellions against the Spanish government, Puerto Ricans finally made a breakthrough in 1897, when Spain issued the Autonomic Charter. It granted Puerto Ricans much more local rule. But in April 1898, just as the island was about to enjoy what amounted to independence from Spain, the Spanish-American War broke out. The conflict lasted less than four months, and the United States was the victor. Spain surrendered its possessions of Puerto Rico, Guam, and the Philippines to the United States.

At first, the island was under U.S. military authority, but over time the United States appointed governors to rule the island.

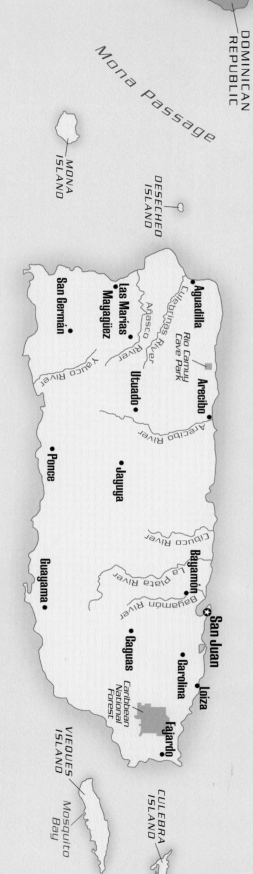

DOMINICAN REPUBLIC

Mona Passage

ATLANTIC OCEAN

CARIBBEAN SEA

MONA ISLAND

DESECHEO ISLAND

Aguadilla

Culebrinas River

Rio Camuy Cave Park

Añasco River

San Germán

Las Marias

Mayagüez

Yauco River

Arecibo

Utuado

Arecibo River

Ponce

Jayuya

Cibuco River

Guayama

Bayamón

La Plata River

Bayamón River

San Juan

Caguas

Carolina

Loiza

Caribbean National Forest

Fajardo

VIEQUES ISLAND

Mosquito Bay

CULEBRA ISLAND

Puerto Rico

International border

● Capital city

⊛ City

0 — 20 KM

0 — 20 Miles

N

UNITED STATES

PACIFIC OCEAN

ATLANTIC OCEAN

CARIBBEAN SEA

PUERTO RICO

COLOMBIA

VENEZUELA

0 — 500 Miles

0 — 500 KM

Then in 1917, the U.S. government passed the Jones Act, declaring Puerto Rico a possession of the United States. The island's residents became U.S. citizens. But Puerto Ricans were denied the right to vote for their own governor until 1948, when they voted Luis Muñoz Marín into office. Soon afterward, they wrote their own constitution, and in 1952, the island became a commonwealth of the United States.

Meanwhile, an economic program called Operation Bootstrap (Operación Manos de Obra) was attracting American corporations to the island. The program shifted the focus of the island's economy from its traditional agricultural base to industry. Puerto Rico's economy came to rely heavily on service industries and manufacturing.

Puerto Rico is an island of contrasts. From quiet rural towns to the bustling streets of the capital of San Juan, Puerto Rico is a unique blend of Taíno, Spanish, and African cultures. Some Puerto Ricans are content with the island's status as a U.S. commonwealth. Others, however, would prefer independence, and some would like to see the island become a state. Only time will tell how the issue of the island's status will be resolved.

THE LAND

In the waters between North and South America, a chain of islands called the West Indies forms a long curve. These islands are made up of three groups—the Greater Antilles, the Lesser Antilles, and the Bahamas. The relatively large islands of Cuba, Jamaica, Hispaniola (Haiti and the Dominican Republic), and Puerto Rico are part of the Greater Antilles.

Of all of the islands that make up the Greater Antilles, Puerto Rico is the smallest and the farthest to the east. Approximately 1,000 miles (1,609 kilometers) southeast of Miami, Florida, the island is surrounded by the deep waters of the Atlantic Ocean to the north and the Caribbean Sea to the south. To the east of Puerto Rico lies the Virgin Passage, which separates the commonwealth from the U.S. Virgin Islands. To the west, the Mona Passage lies between Puerto Rico and the Dominican Republic.

With an area of 3,515 square miles (9,104 square km), Puerto Rico is slightly smaller than the state of Connecticut. But the island's

population of 3,808,670 is large for its size. In fact, Puerto Rico is one of the most densely populated areas in the world. According to the U.S. Census Bureau, Puerto Rico averages more than 1,100 people per square mile (440 people per sq. km).

The main island of Puerto Rico has a rectangular shape, and it measures approximately 100 miles by 35 miles (161 km by 56 km). The Commonwealth of Puerto Rico, as it is officially called, also includes three smaller islands: Mona to the west, Culebra and Vieques to the east, and many smaller islets. Puerto Rico is the largest of all the U.S. territories.

The island of Vieques had long been the center of a controversy. The U.S. Navy had owned two-thirds of that island and had used the property to conduct land and sea training exercises for more than sixty years. Vieques residents strongly disapproved of the navy's presence, citing ecological damage and noise pollution as the result of the bombing exercises. In 1978 Vieques's fishing crews protested by sailing forty fishing boats into island waters where the navy had planned target practice using live ammunition. In 1999 a Puerto Rican guard on the bombing range was accidentally killed. This again sparked opposition to the navy's presence, and protesters descended on the range. The U.S. Navy withdrew from Vieques on May 1, 2003, turning over the island's eastern third to the U.S. Department of the Interior and moving their training exercises to the U.S. mainland.

Topography

Puerto Rico has a surprising variety of landscapes for its relatively small area. The island's diverse geographical features range from rugged mountains to coastal plains and from dense, tropical rain forests to palm-fringed beaches with powder-fine sand.

From east to west across the middle of the island, the Cordillera Central forms a wide, mountainous backbone. Peaks generally range from 1,000 to 3,000 feet (305 to 915 meters) above sea level. The island's highest mountain, Cerro de Punta, which rises 4,389 feet (1,338 m), is part of this range. In the northeast, the Luquillo Mountains, a smaller chain, features El Yunque, a 3,483-foot (1,062-m) peak in the Caribbean National Forest. Another small chain, the Sierra de Cayey, is located in the southeast.

The Caribbean National Forest is often called **El Yunque,** which is the name of a mountain found within the park.

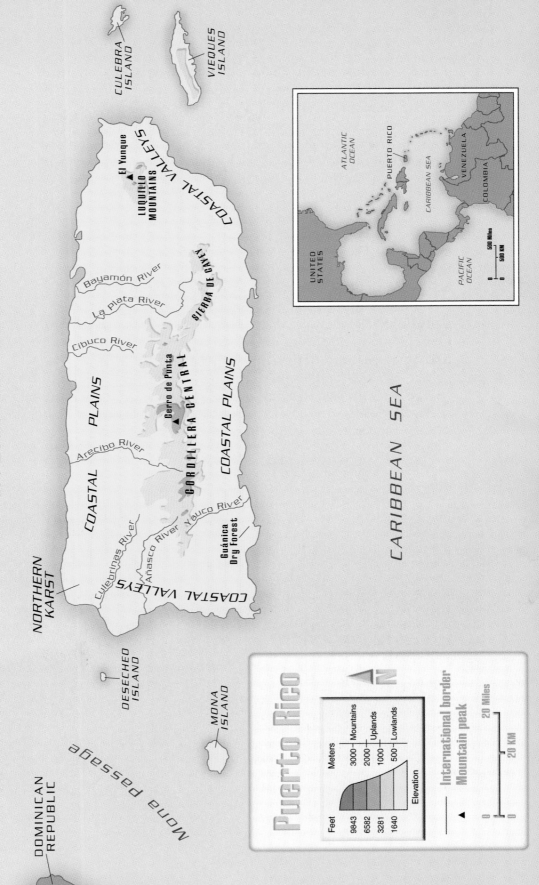

ATLANTIC · OCEAN

CULEBRA ISLAND

VIEQUES ISLAND

ATLANTIC OCEAN

PUERTO RICO

CARIBBEAN SEA

VENEZUELA

COLOMBIA

UNITED STATES

PACIFIC OCEAN

500 Miles

500 KM

El Yunque

LUQUILLO MOUNTAINS

COASTAL VALLEYS

Bayamón River

La plata River

SIERRA DE CAYEY

Cibuco River

Cerro de Punta

CORDILLERA CENTRAL

COASTAL PLAINS

COASTAL PLAINS

Arecibo River

Yauco River

COASTAL

Añasco River

Guánica Dry Forest

Culebrinas River

COASTAL VALLEYS

NORTHERN KARST

DESECHEO ISLAND

MONA ISLAND

DOMINICAN REPUBLIC

Mona passage

CARIBBEAN SEA

Puerto Rico

N

International border

Mountain peak

Feet	Meters	
9843	3000	Mountains
6582	2000	Uplands
3281	1000	
1640	500	Lowlands

Elevation

20 Miles

20 KM

Long, narrow coastal plains rim the northern and southern sides of the island. In the rich coastal valleys of eastern and western Puerto Rico, sugarcane and other crops thrive.

The karst region in the northwest, which features unusual, conical limestone formations called *mogotes* (Spanish for "haystack hills"), is one of the island's most unique areas. These haystack hills rise up in the otherwise stark landscape. Mogotes take centuries to form. Rainfall gradually erodes and dissolves the limestone terrain, forming sinkholes. The pieces of limestone that remain between the sinkholes are the haystack hills. Deep caves and underground lakes also form as a result of this geological action. One extensive network of caves is protected within Río Camuy Cave Park, which features a 180-foot (55-m) high cave.

The Puerto Rico Trench, a depression in the ocean floor, lies north of the island. Part of the trench reaches more than 28,000 feet (8,534 m) and is one of the deepest areas of the Atlantic Ocean. Geologists say that the islands in the Greater Antilles are the tops of a submerged mountain chain.

Rivers and Lakes

Puerto Rico's longest rivers originate in the mountains and flow north into the Atlantic Ocean. Only one river on the island, the Rio Grande de Loíza, can be navigated by large vessels. Other large rivers include the Arecibo, La Plata, and the Añasco. The Río Camuy flows underground through a massive cave network on the northern side of the island. The Río Camuy is the third largest underground river in the world.

The placid **Añasco River** flows through a forest in western Puerto Rico.

Puerto Rico has no natural lakes, but dams have created a number of reservoirs (lakes or ponds in which water is stored). These bodies of water are used for irrigation and to produce hydroelectricity.

Climate

Puerto Rico has a pleasant, sunny climate year-round. The island lies within the tropics, an area defined by the Tropic of Cancer north of the equator and the Tropic of Capricorn south of the equator. Within the tropics, the sun shines most intensely on the earth's surface and typically produces hot and humid conditions. Despite the island's tropical location, trade winds from the east keep temperatures in the mild 70° to 80°F (21° to 27°C) range. More rainfall occurs in the lush, green northern part of the island than in the arid south. The rain forest at El Yunque receives as much as 200 inches (508 centimeters) of rain each year.

Destructive hurricanes can pass through the Caribbean between June and November. Some severe hurricanes have struck Puerto Rico. Hurricane David came in 1979, and Hurricane Hugo swept through in 1989. Hurricane Georges, with wind speeds of 115 miles per hour

Hurricane Georges caused much damage to the island in 1998. Although the climate is typically calm and warm, powerful tropical storms sometimes sweep across Puerto Rico, leaving a trail of destruction.

(185 km per hour), struck in 1998. Georges caused power outages and millions of dollars' worth of damage to the island's airports and piers.

Flora and Fauna

Tropical rain forests once covered the island, but most have been cut down to clear the land for agriculture and human settlement. About three thousand species of plants, including many unique trees, still flourish there.

The *flamboyán*, or royal poinciana, features blazing reddish orange blossoms. Fast-growing trees, such as ceiba or kapok trees, bamboo trees, and palm trees, take root in the island's rich soil, along with hardwoods such as the satinwood, Spanish elm, mahogany, and rare *ausubo* trees. The ausubo does not rot or attract termites, and many of the historic buildings in the old section of San Juan were built with beams made from this hardy tree. Mangrove swamps lie along the coast, while the Guánica Dry Forest in the southwest features hundreds of varieties of cactus and other desert plants. Colorful flowers such as the *maga*, or Puerto Rican hibiscus, and pink oleander also thrive on the island, and when in bloom, the sweet fragrances of jasmine and gardenia fill the air.

The 28,000-acre (11,331-hectare) Caribbean National Forest, popularly known as El Yunque, is the only tropical rain forest within the

The strikingly red **flamboyán** is sometimes called the flame tree in English.

Mist rises from an area of **tropical rain forest** in the Caribbean National Forest.

U.S. National Forest system. Its lush interior sustains approximately 240 types of trees, of which 23 can only be found in this forest. In addition, the rain forest is home to more than 150 species of ferns and 50 types of orchids.

One of the rarest species of bird in the world, the Puerto Rican parrot, is found only in El Yunque. Puerto Rico's colorful, tropical birds also include the *reinita* (Spanish for "little queen"), the island's unofficial bird.

Bats, iguanas and other lizards, some nonpoisonous snakes, guinea pigs, and mongooses also live on the island. Perhaps the most famous and most beloved animal in Puerto Rico is the *coquí.* Found almost no place else in the world, the tiny tree frog sings its nighttime serenade, which sounds like "co-KEE."

Barracuda, mullet, tuna, and lobsters are among the marine animals that thrive in Puerto Rico's waters. Jellyfish and multicolored tropical fish such as the blue parrot fish can be spotted in the coral reefs off the island's coasts.

Puerto Rico is also a haven for rare and endangered species. A strange species of blind fish is

Coquí

found only in the underground river that flows through Río Camuy Cave Park. Rare leatherback turtles nest on the smaller island of Culebra, and Vieques is home to wild horses. Mona Island, almost 50 miles (80 km) to the west of the main island, is a protected area. No people live on Mona, but some rare animals, including large lizards called Mona iguanas, make their homes there. Exotic birds such as the red-footed booby also inhabit the small island.

Natural Resources

When the Spaniards colonized the island in the 1500s, they enslaved the early inhabitants and forced them to mine gold. This quickly depleted most of Puerto Rico's gold resources. In modern times, deposits of copper, nickel, and other minerals remain. The limestone that is mined in Puerto Rico is used in the production of cement.

Cities

Puerto Rico's cities range from quaint fishing towns to sprawling modern cities that are centers of manufacturing and trade. Most of the island's residents live in cities. About one-third of the population resides in the metropolitan area of San Juan, the capital city. San Juan,

Ponce, and Mayagüez are three of the largest cities. Other important cities include Caguas and Arecibo.

SAN JUAN Located on the northeastern Atlantic coast, San Juan is by far the island's largest city. Although San Juan lies in a flat, coastal area, mountains frame the city on the east and south. More than 430,000 people live in central San Juan, but the population of the Greater San Juan metropolitan area is approximately 1 million. It is a bustling, densely populated area that includes picturesque neighborhoods with colonial buildings.

The Spanish explorer Juan Ponce de León founded Puerto Rico's first European settlement at nearby Caparra in 1508, and he later became the first governor of the island. In 1521 the capital city moved to the site of present-day San Juan. The city was first called Puerto Rico, or "rich port." The island itself was named San Juan Bautista (Saint John the Baptist). Eventually, the island and the city exchanged names. The city became San Juan, and the island was called Puerto Rico.

Old San Juan (Viejo San Juan), the original walled city, is situated on a peninsula northwest of the modern city of San Juan. El Morro, an

San Juan, the second oldest city in the Americas, is home to one of the biggest and best natural harbors in the Caribbean. Visit vgsbooks.com to find information on what to see and do in San Juan, what the weather is like there, and more.

The massive walls of **El Morro,** a fortress built in the sixteenth century, still adorn the landscape of Old San Juan.

impressive fortress built by the Spaniards in the 1540s, protected the city from invasion. With cobblestone streets, antique gates, and a picturesque promenade, Old San Juan blends the architecture of colonial Spain with the modern architecture of other parts of the city.

Coffee, tobacco, sugar, and other products are exported from San Juan's harbor. The city is Puerto Rico's chief commercial area, in addition to serving as the island's intellectual and cultural center. The University of Puerto Rico and countless museums and art galleries are all located in San Juan. Each June San Juan hosts the Casals Festival at the Luis A. Ferré Performing Arts Center. The festival lasts for ten days and features classical music performances in honor of the late cellist Pablo Casals, a former resident of Old San Juan.

The city is also home to a thriving tourist industry supported by the luxurious hotels situated on sparkling white beaches. Major cruise lines that sail through the Caribbean make stops in San Juan so passengers can enjoy a day or two in the lively city.

PONCE Ponce, with a population of 186,475, is the island's second largest city. Situated on the southern coast of Puerto Rico, it faces the Caribbean and is also a frequent port for cruise ships. Known as "the pearl of the South," sunny Ponce is filled with impressive public

Vendors and shoppers talk shop in an open-air market in Ponce.

buildings and beautiful homes. Visitors enjoy free trolleys and horse-drawn carriage rides around the main plaza.

The Ponce Museum of Art is one of the city's most famous attractions. Designed by Edward Durrell Stone, the architect of the Museum of Modern Art in New York City, the building is the largest art museum in the Caribbean. Its collection includes more than two thousand works by local and international artists.

Ponce's industries include tourism and the canning and processing of agricultural products. Ponce's shipping industry exports coffee, tobacco, and tropical fruits to other countries. Ponce's manufactured items include electrical devices, textiles, shoes, and cement.

MAYAGÜEZ On the western coast of Puerto Rico lies Mayagüez, population 98,475, another important shipping city. During the winter months, the beautiful beaches that surround the city are a great place to watch the humpback whales that migrate to the area.

Founded in 1760, the city's name is Taíno for "place of great waters." Mayagüez has survived two immense disasters. In 1841 a huge fire swept through the city's center. Then in 1918, a tremendous earthquake devastated the city.

Mayagüez has always sprung back, and the modern city features an impressive plaza with a monument to Christopher Columbus surrounded by sixteen bronze statues. Mayagüez is a modern manufacturing center where products such as pharmaceuticals and electronic components are made.

On the outskirts of the city, the Tropical Agriculture Research Station, which was founded in 1901, features a collection of more than two thousand exotic plants, including rubber, coffee, and coconut trees. The station conducts research on a variety of agricultural topics, including how to grow tropical food crops more efficiently.

HISTORY AND GOVERNMENT

Before the arrival of Europeans and long before there was a sprawling metropolis known as San Juan, Puerto Rico was a beautiful, untouched island filled with tropical greenery, soaring mountains, multicolored plants, and cascading waterfalls. Little is known about the very first inhabitants of the island, but archaeologists—scientists who learn about ancient cultures by studying artifacts dug up from the ground—refer to them as the Archaics. Some archeologists think that the first islanders came from what would later become Florida.

Around the first century A.D., people—probably from what would later be called Venezuela—arrived on the island. Known as the Igneri people, these newcomers were members of the Arawak language group. Some archaeologists believe that these inhabitants were the beginning of what would eventually evolve into the Ostionoid culture. Yet other archaeologists propose that an entirely new wave of people migrated to Puerto Rico from South America, conquering the people who lived on the island at the time.

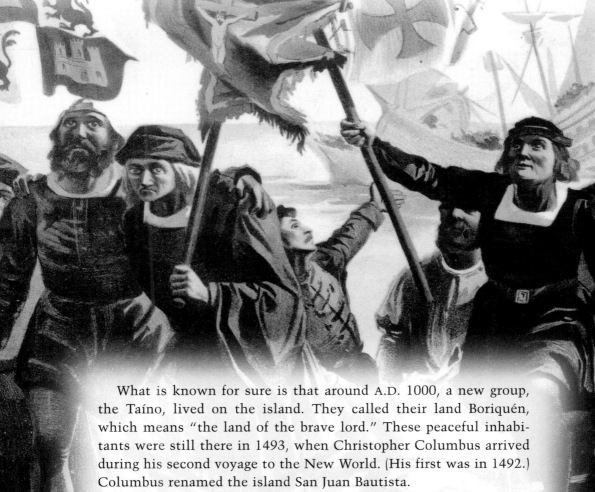

What is known for sure is that around A.D. 1000, a new group, the Taíno, lived on the island. They called their land Boriquén, which means "the land of the brave lord." These peaceful inhabitants were still there in 1493, when Christopher Columbus arrived during his second voyage to the New World. (His first was in 1492.) Columbus renamed the island San Juan Bautista.

Columbus, an Italian-born navigator who had been seeking an ocean route to India, was under the sponsorship of Queen Isabella of Spain. Instead of arriving in Asia, Columbus sailed through the Caribbean Sea.

Columbus and his crew observed how the Taínos lived. Each village had a *cacique* (chief); nobles called *nitaínos,* who functioned as advisers to the chiefs; commoners; and *naborías* (slaves). The priests were called *bohiques.* The Taínos lived in round houses called *bohíos* that were made of palm or sugarcane stalks that had been tied together with rattan and covered with thatched roofs. These houses were built

The Taínos built and lived in huts called **bohíos,** which were constructed of bundles of reeds.

around a central plaza called a *batey*. The Taínos were good farmers, and they also cultivated beautiful gardens.

Excellent rowers and navigators, the Taínos built wooden canoes that could accommodate as many as eighty people. They lived on islands throughout the Caribbean Sea, and they were especially well established in what would later be called the Dominican Republic. Near the sea, the Taínos had built a tall watchtower from which to watch for possible invasion by the Caribs, fierce warriors who lived throughout the area.

The Taínos were skilled woodcarvers and weavers. They crafted jewelry and plates from gold that they found in riverbeds. The

Taíno canoes were large and sturdy, providing an easy means of transportation between the islands of the Caribbean.

presence of gold immediately caught Columbus's eye.

Spanish Settlers

During the 1500s, Spain became the strongest power in Europe, primarily because of Columbus's voyages to the New World. By 1508 the Spaniards had established a permanent settlement, or colony, on the island. Juan Ponce de León, who had participated in Columbus's second voyage, led a small group of settlers to found the town of Caparra on the north shore of the island. Agueybana, the island's Taíno cacique, or chief, welcomed the settlers. In 1509 the Spanish government appointed Juan Ponce de León as the island's first governor.

In 1519 the Spaniards abandoned Caparra and reestablished a city at the site of present-day San Juan. They renamed the city Puerto Rico. In 1521 the town and the island switched names.

Although the Spaniards were initially friendly toward the Taínos, their greed for gold made them turn on the original inhabitants. The Spaniards forced the Taínos to mine for gold and to farm the land. Taíno men were often separated from their families and brought to work in mines far from home. They were underfed, receiving only cassava, bread, and an occasional bit of pork while laboring long and hard.

In addition, the Spaniards, who were Roman Catholics, insisted on converting the Taínos to their own religion. They demanded that the sons of Taíno chiefs leave their

GIFTS OF THE TAÍNOS

The peaceful natives that Columbus encountered on Puerto Rico left a rich legacy. They slept in hanging beds called *hamacas*. These comfortable creations became known as "hammocks," although most people don't realize that we owe both the name and the invention to Puerto Rico's first inhabitants.

The musical instruments used by native people have also survived in the Caribbean and in Latin America. Maracas, drums, and güiro (pronounced "gwee-ro")—a grooved gourd that makes a scratchy sound when a stick is scraped across it—all came from the Taínos.

Taíno religion included a benevolent deity named Yukiyú, who protected the people. But there was also an evil deity named Juracán, who often unleashed violent storms on the island. Our word for these treacherous storms, "hurricane," derives from the name of the malevolent Taíno spirit.

The names of some modern Puerto Rican cities such as Mayagüez, Humacao, and Caguas also come from the Taínos. Puerto Ricans often refer to themselves as *boricuas*, people from the island the Taínos called Boriquén.

This sixteenth-century drawing shows **Taínos forced to dig for gold** by their Spanish captors.

families at the age of thirteen to live with missionaries to learn about the Catholic religion. The natives, increasingly unhappy with how the Spaniards were treating them, led several unsuccessful rebellions against their captors. But the bows and arrows of the natives were no match for the firearms and swords of the Spaniards.

By the end of the 1500s, the harsh treatment and unintentionally introduced diseases such as measles and smallpox had wiped out most of the Taíno population. Meanwhile, with the decline in the Taíno workforce, the Spaniards began to import African slaves to perform manual labor.

Attacks on the Island

Although the island initially held the promise of being a source of great wealth for the Spanish Empire, the gold mines had been depleted by the 1530s. But Spanish ships, filled with treasures from other Spanish colonies in Mexico and present-day Latin America, often stopped in Puerto Rico en route to Spain. Puerto Rico was also the first stop for all Spanish ships in the Caribbean. Anchored off Puerto Rico's shores, these ships attracted the attention of pirates in the area. Puerto Rico, which is strategically located at the center of the Caribbean, was also attracting the attention of the English and the French, both of whom sought possession of the island so they could expand their rule in the New World. In addition, the warlike Caribs frequently raided Puerto Rico, taking island women back with them.

Because of these attacks, the Spaniards realized the need for strong fortifications and made plans to build forts. La Fortaleza (also called Santa Catalina) was completed in 1540. Soon after, construction began on El Castillo de San Felipe del Morro, popularly known as El Morro. In the late 1500s, the Spaniards erected more defenses, including the forts of El Boquerón and Santa Elena.

By the end of the 1500s, Spain's influence as a world power was declining. Then in 1585, a war broke out between Spain and England. Although the ships of the Spanish Armada, Spain's naval fleet, were known to be the most powerful at the time, the English defeated Spain in 1588, striking a terrible blow to the Spanish Empire. Despite further attacks by the English, Spain held on to Puerto Rico, even into the 1600s, when the Dutch launched an attack on the island.

In the 1600s and 1700s, Spain did not allow Puerto Rico to trade with any other countries, and only the port of San Juan was to be used. These economic policies effectively shut down foreign trade.

But British, French, Danish, and Dutch traders found a way around Spain's ban. They smuggled goods in and out of Puerto Rico, far from San Juan, out of sight of the island's Spanish rulers. The island's residents exchanged their cattle, sugarcane, fruits, tobacco, and other products for slaves and manufactured goods, which they received from

Tobacco, here being prepared for sale in the 1900s, was one of the products that Puerto Ricans traded to Europeans in the 1600s and 1700s.

their illegal trading partners. Coastal towns such as Arecibo, Aguada, and Fajardo became profitable smuggling centers.

Longing for Independence

In the 1800s, many Puerto Ricans wanted to break free from Spain. Because of Spain's refusal to abolish slavery and its enforcement of curfews and banning of certain books, Puerto Rican activists started a movement for self-government.

One of the leaders of the independence movement was Ramón Emeterio Betances, a medical doctor who became a revolutionary. He wrote "The Ten Commandments of Free Men," and his ideas formed the very roots of the independence movement. Among his ten demands were the call for the abolition of slavery and the right of men to elect their own governing officials.

Because of his revolutionary views, Spanish authorities exiled Betances from Puerto Rico. But that did not stop him. He moved to Europe, then on to the Dominican Republic, and eventually to New York City, all the while expanding his ideas of liberating Puerto Rico from Spanish rule. His intent was to raise money and gather supporters for a major rebellion against the Spanish government. Throughout Puerto Rico, secret societies sprang up to aid the rebellion.

On the night of September 23, 1868, about six hundred revolutionaries marched into the town of Lares shouting "Death to Spain, long live liberty, long live free Puerto Rico." This rebellion became known as El Grito de Lares, or "The Shout of Lares." But the uprising did not go as planned. Someone reported the secret plot to the

Ramón Emeterio Betances was one of the founders of the Puerto Rican independence movement.

Spanish authorities, and eventually the Spaniards quelled the revolution, jailing hundreds of rebels. In present-day Puerto Rico, September 23 is a national holiday, and Betances is hailed as a hero in his native land.

Giving in to the pressures of the nationalist movement in Puerto Rico, Spain abolished slavery in 1873. Then in 1897, Spain passed the Autonomic Charter, a document that granted the island a great deal of local rule. The efforts of Luis Muñoz Rivera, an influential journalist and politician, helped make the charter possible. Puerto Rico had finally achieved much of the independence that its residents had so long desired. But in May 1898, just as Muñoz Rivera was about to lead a newly formed government and just as Puerto Rico was poised to practice self-rule, the Spanish-American War erupted.

The Spanish-American War

The Spanish-American War officially began on April 25, 1898. Spain and the United States were in conflict over several issues, including U.S. insistence that Cuba should gain its independence from Spain.

On July 25, 1898, a U.S. fleet led by General Nelson A. Miles invaded Guánica and later Ponce, both in southern Puerto Rico. After a number of battles in Puerto Rico, the Philippines, and Cuba, the United States won the war in August 1898. Under the Treaty of Paris, which was signed on December 10, 1898, Spain surrendered its possessions of Puerto Rico, Guam, and the Philippines to the United States. (Under the treaty, Spain granted freedom to Cuba.)

Nelson A. Miles

By this time, Puerto Rico was already densely populated with close to one million residents, the majority of whom lived in rural areas. Puerto Ricans had mixed reactions to the U.S. takeover. Initially, Muñoz Rivera urged people to resist yet another foreign rule. From exile in France, Betances called for revolutionary measures for the island to keep its newfound independence. Others gladly welcomed the presence of the U.S. government. They appreciated the protection and freedoms enjoyed by the United States, such as the freedom of the press. They also looked forward to doing business and gaining profits from trade with the United States.

U.S. Rule

From 1898 until 1900, Puerto Rico was under the rule of the U.S. military. Then in 1900, the United States passed the First Organic Act of Puerto Rico, also known as the Foraker Act. This established how the island would be governed. U.S. president William McKinley appointed a governor to the island, and the U.S. Supreme Court had ultimate power over the Puerto Rican justice system. The Foraker Act established the policy that Puerto Rico "belongs to the United States, but it is not the United States, nor a part of the United States."

Meanwhile, the Puerto Rican independence movement continued to grow. Luis Muñoz Rivera became Puerto Rico's representative in Washington, D.C., where he tirelessly campaigned for the United States to extend the rights of Puerto Ricans. Finally, on March 2, 1917, U.S. president Woodrow Wilson signed into law the Second Organic Act, also called the Jones Act. It replaced the Foraker Act and stated that Puerto Rico was a possession of the United States, and as a result, it granted U.S. citizenship to the people of Puerto Rico. The act also established a legislature modeled on that of the United States consisting of two parts, a House of Representatives and a Senate. Puerto Ricans would elect both the senators and the representatives.

Although some viewed the Jones Act as a step forward, many Puerto Ricans still felt politically constrained. Under the Jones Act, the president of the United States still appointed the governor of Puerto Rico, all the Supreme Court justices, and other political decision makers on the island.

Puerto Rico objected to other provisions of the Jones Act, including the appointment of an auditor. This official's job was to examine all the accounts of the Puerto Rican government. In addition, another U.S.-appointed official, the commissioner of education, was to establish rules for appointing teachers and selecting the courses of study that would be implemented throughout the island.

But Puerto Rico also experienced progress in some highly needed areas. The introduction of better hospitals, schools, sanitation systems, dams, and roads improved the quality of life. For example,

Many Puerto Ricans objected to parts of the Jones Act. However, U.S. aid made possible the construction of new **hospitals,** like this one in Ponce, and other public buildings and works.

61 - HOSPITAL DE TUBERCULOSOS, PONCE.
COPR. RODRIGUEZ SERRA, PONCE

just eleven years after the U.S. takeover, the number of schools in Puerto Rico more than doubled from 874 to 1,912. But the island's economy was still dependent on agriculture, and U.S. companies owned and ran the most profitable plantations and sugar mills. These American companies, not the people of Puerto Rico, profited most from the U.S. presence. As a result of the improvements in sanitation, the population increased.

In the 1930s, when the market for sugar decreased, Puerto Rico was hard hit. During the Great Depression (1929–1939), Puerto Rico felt the negative impact of the worldwide economic slump. Unemployment increased, and many people were close to starvation during these difficult years.

In 1938 the U.S. Navy began using Vieques for military exercises. In 1941 the navy forced some of the residents of Vieques to move from their homes. This gave the navy possession of more than two-thirds of the island. To learn more about the Vieques controversy from the point of view of the island's residents, log onto vgsbooks.com.

In 1933 Franklin Delano Roosevelt became president of the United States. His assistant secretary of agriculture was Rexford Tugwell, an American economist and political scientist. In 1941 Roosevelt appointed him as the governor of Puerto Rico, and in 1943, Tugwell recommended that the United States allow Puerto Ricans to elect their own governors.

This goal was not achieved immediately. In 1946 Roosevelt's successor, Harry S. Truman appointed Jesús Piñero, a prominent politician, as the first Puerto Rican-born governor of the island. In 1948 Puerto Ricans chose Luis Muñoz Marín, son of Luis Muñoz Rivera, as the first popularly elected governor of Puerto Rico.

After living for years under the rule of governors appointed by the United States, Puerto Ricans chose **Luis Muñoz Marín** as their first elected leader.

LUIS MUÑOZ MARÍN

One of the most influential politicians in Puerto Rico's history was Luis Muñoz Marín. The son of Luis Muñoz Rivera, he was born in Puerto Rico but raised in the United States because of his father's position as the island's representative. Consequently, Muñoz Marín was fluent in both English and Spanish. He attended Georgetown University in Washington, D.C., before returning to his homeland. In 1938 he created Puerto Rico's Popular Democratic Party, which strived to address the island's economic problems. In 1946 Muñoz Marín began thinking of an option besides possible statehood or independence for Puerto Rico. The Commonwealth of Puerto Rico was the result. In 1948 he became Puerto Rico's first popularly elected governor and held that post until 1964.

Muñoz Marín had spearheaded an economic program that started in the 1940s and continued for two decades. Known as Operation Bootstrap, the program transformed Puerto Rico's economy from agriculture to industry, mostly by offering tax exemptions to U.S. companies that invested their own money to build factories on the island.

As one of the founders of the Popular Democratic Party, Muñoz Marín was a staunch advocate of social and economic reform. His party's slogan was "Bread, Land, and Liberty," and posters for the party displayed a picture of a *jíbaro*—a poor, rural farmer from the mountainous countryside of Puerto Rico—with a traditional broad-brimmed hat. Muñoz Marín also strongly supported the concept of making Puerto Rico a commonwealth, or self-governing territory.

On July 3, 1950, the U.S. Congress approved Public Law 600, which granted Puerto Ricans the right to create their own constitution, including a Bill of Rights. A Puerto Rican convention wrote the constitution, which was similar to that of the United States, and the island's people approved it.

This poster displays the slogan of Puerto Rico's Popular Democratic Party, **"Bread, Land, and Liberty."**

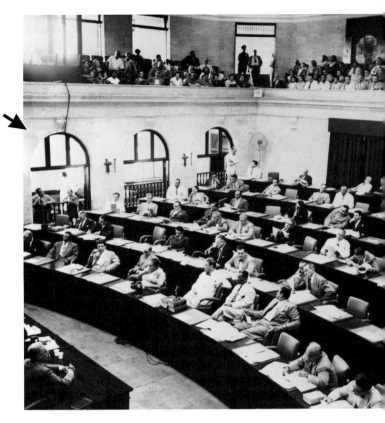

It took about five months for the Puerto Rican legislature to write and approve Puerto Rico's constitution. Here the legislators begin the final **Constitutional Assembly** session. Governor Luis Muñoz Marín sits in the center of the front row.

Many Puerto Ricans were pleased with this arrangement, but the Puerto Rican Nationalist Party still wanted independence for the island. On November 1, 1950, two Puerto Rican revolutionaries attempted to assassinate President Harry S. Truman. After a shootout with security guards, one police officer was killed, but the president was safe. One of the revolutionaries died in the fight.

On July 25, 1952, the fifty-fourth anniversary of the U.S. invasion of Puerto Rico, Governor Luis Muñoz Marín declared the island's new status as Estado Libre Asociado, or "free associated state." The term has been translated into English as "commonwealth of the United States" to stress that the island is not a state, but rather a self-governing possession of the United States.

On March 1, 1954, the Nationalist Party again protested Puerto Rico's commonwealth status. Four of the party's members—Lolita Lebrón, Irwin Flores, Rafael Cancel Miranda, and Andrés Figueroa—entered the U.S. House of Representatives in Washington, D.C. Lebrón unfurled the Puerto Rican flag and shouted, "Viva Puerto Rico libre!" ("Long live a free Puerto Rico!"). Flores and Cancel Miranda opened fire, and five congressmen were wounded. (The four party members subsequently served twenty-five years in federal prisons.)

A GROUNDBREAKING GOVERNOR

The first female governor of Puerto Rico, Sila Calderón, took office in January 2001. She brought a wealth of experience to her new job. Born and raised in San Juan, she received a B.A. in political science and an M.A. in public administration and later served as the president of an investment firm. In the 1970s, she worked as special assistant to Rafael Hernández Colón, then governor of the island. She also became Puerto Rico's first female chief of staff in 1984. In 1988 Governor Colón appointed her as the first female secretary of state. She was elected mayor of San Juan in 1996. Sila Calderón was staunchly opposed to the U.S. Navy's presence in Vieques but favors commonwealth status.

Muñoz Marín, Puerto Rico's governor for four terms, announced in 1964 that he would not run for another term. Roberto Sánchez Vilella, who was in favor of Puerto Rico's commonwealth status, became the new governor in 1965. In 1967 he held a plebiscite—a vote on a specific issue—which asked islanders their views on the island's status. The overwhelming majority was in favor of the current commonwealth status. The next governor, Luis A. Ferré, favored statehood. From then onward, a succession of governors have alternated between favoring commonwealth status or favoring statehood.

◉ Recent Events

Two important issues have dominated the politics of modern Puerto Rico—the island's political status and the U.S. Navy's presence in Vieques, the small island that lies to the east of the main island of Puerto Rico. The question of Puerto Rico's status is still unanswered. The Popular Democratic Party is in favor of retaining commonwealth status but with some changes. The New Progressive Party (PNP) wants Puerto Rico to become the fifty-first state. Another less influential party, the Puerto Rican Independence Party (PIP), would like to break political ties with the United States altogether.

In 1993 another vote held on the status question produced a pro-commonwealth result. But the outcome of a third vote in 1998 was surprising. Among the choices on the ballot were statehood, commonwealth status, and "none of the above." Just over 50 percent of the voters marked their ballots with "none of the above." Members of the Popular Democratic Party said that they voted this way to protest how the commonwealth was defined. The statehood option received 46 percent of the vote. The question of Puerto Rico's status is still open to debate.

The other highly controversial issue was whether the U.S. Navy should be allowed to stay on the island of Vieques and carry out bombing exercises. The navy said it needed these practice bombings to prepare for possible warfare. The area was the largest U.S. naval site where it was possible to practice using ships, planes, and underwater craft. The navy operated a bombing range of 900 acres (364 hectares) on the eastern tip of the island.

Opposition to the navy's military exercises grew when a bomb accidentally killed David Sanes Rodríguez, a civilian guard, on April 19, 1999. Marine jets had unintentionally dropped a bomb on an observation tower where the guard was stationed. Protesters camped out on restricted areas of naval property and demanded that the bombing cease immediately. The protest stopped the exercises for one year.

But on May 4, 2000, federal authorities started arresting the protesters, including Damaso Serrano, the mayor of Vieques, for trespassing on U.S. Navy property. Serrano spent four months in federal prison in San Juan. Four prominent New Yorkers were arrested and became known as the Vieques Four: Adolfo Carrión Jr., a New York City councilman;

Handcuffed protesters raise their arms while waiting to be loaded into trucks after being arrested by U.S. marshals on May 4, 2000, at Camp Garcia in Vieques. The marshals arrested about sixty people for blocking the gate to the base as a protest against the navys' use of the site for a bombing range.

Roberto Ramirez, the Bronx County Democratic Committee chairman; José Rivera, a New York State assemblyman; and the Reverend Al Sharpton, who went on a hunger strike when he was in prison.

President George W. Bush responded by agreeing to look for alternative sites. On May 1, 2003, the navy withdrew from the area. The land was turned over to the U.S. Department of the Interior, which will decide whether the land is to be designated for civilian use or as a wildlife refuge. At the stroke of midnight, thousands of jubilant Vieques residents gathered at the U.S. naval base and ripped down the gate that separated navy holdings from the rest of the island. Although the navy is gone, Vieques residents still voice concerns over the cleanup of their land, which is still contaminated by chemicals given off during bombing exercises.

To learn more about Puerto Rico's history, including information on the Tainos, the debate over the island's relationship with the United States, and much more, go to vgsbooks.com.

Government

The Commonwealth of Puerto Rico is part of the U.S. federal system. Although Puerto Ricans are citizens of the United States, their island is not a state, and the people cannot vote for the president of the United States. However, they are allowed to vote in the primaries staged by the Democratic and the Republican Parties. In the primaries, registered members of those parties choose which candidates will run for office.

Under the commonwealth system, Puerto Ricans can vote in elections for government offices on the island. The island has a representative—called a resident commissioner—in the U.S. Congress. Although the commissioner participates in the proceedings, he or she is not allowed to vote in Congress. Laws passed by the U.S. Congress generally apply to Puerto Rico as well as to the states.

Puerto Ricans may serve in the U.S. armed forces and many of them fought in the Korean War and the Vietnam War. The United States is in charge of the island's foreign affairs. The islanders are not required to pay federal income tax, which all residents of the United States must do. The United States gives Puerto Rico more than $13 billion in federal funds annually.

Puerto Rico has one of the highest rates of voter participation in the world.

Puerto Rico has its own constitution, which is similar to the U.S. Constitution. The island's

Puerto Rico's Legislative Assembly meets in the Capitol Building in San Juan.

government is divided into three branches: the executive, the legislative, and the judicial. Puerto Ricans vote for their own governor and for their senators and representatives. The executive authority is the governor, who is elected for a four-year term. There is no limit as to how many terms the governor may serve if elected again by the voters.

The legislative branch of the Puerto Rican government is comprised of the Senate and the House of Representatives. There are twenty-seven senators and fifty-one members of the House of Representatives. If one of the two major parties—the Popular Democratic Party or the New Progressive Party—controls more than two-thirds of the seats in the Legislative Assembly, the number of seats for the minority party will be increased in accordance with the Puerto Rican Constitution to prevent the majority party from dominating all votes.

Judicial power is vested in the Puerto Rican Supreme Court and the lower courts. The governor nominates the chief justice and associate justices, and the Senate confirms their appointments. The U.S. president nominates the seven judges of Puerto Rico's federal district court, and the U.S. Senate confirms all nominees. Decisions made by the Puerto Rican Supreme Court may be appealed and taken to the U.S. Supreme Court.

THE PEOPLE

The people of Puerto Rico have a wonderful diversity of ethnic backgrounds. Together they create a culture that is unique to the island. After the Spaniards arrived and colonized Puerto Rico, the native Taínos eventually died out, but some of them had married Spaniards and African slaves. Most modern Puerto Ricans are a mixture of Indian, African, and European heritages.

In addition to the Spanish colonists, Europeans from countries such as France, Scotland, and Ireland came to the island in the early 1800s. Later in the nineteenth century, when roads were built, workers from China, Italy, and Germany moved to Puerto Rico and settled on the island. They left their homelands in search of higher wages, and the salaries and steady work in Puerto Rico were better than those offered in their native lands. The beautiful island and its sunny weather encouraged people to stay there permanently. In the 1960s, after Fidel Castro took control of Cuba, many Cubans fled to Puerto Rico. People from the Dominican Republic have also come to live in Puerto Rico.

○ A Crowded Island

About one-third of Puerto Rico's 3.8 million people crowd the metropolitan area around San Juan. Seventy-three percent of the island's people live in urban areas. For its relatively small size, the island is highly populated, with 1,100 people per square mile (440 people per sq. km). This population density is one of the highest in the world and much greater than that of the United States. For example, Connecticut, which is slightly larger than Puerto Rico, has only 703 people per square mile (239 people per sq. km)—less than half the density of the island. In the United States, the average population per square mile is only 80 (30 people per sq. km).

Puerto Rico's population is growing steadily. In 1898 when the United States took over the island, the population was about one million. But by 1980, advances in medicine and a high birthrate had raised the population to more than three million. Over the years, the population has continued to grow. If the population continues to

Many of Puerto Rico's cities suffer from urban crowding. Heavy traffic, jam-packed sidewalks, and narrow apartment buildings illustrate this problem.

increase at the current rate, island residents will be forced to either move or take over more ground by cutting down precious natural resources such as forests. There would be more traffic, and consequently, more roads would have to be built. The projected population of Puerto Rico in 2025 is 4.2 million. Another 2.5 million Puerto Ricans live on the U.S. mainland, mostly on the East Coast. Nearly 800,000 of them reside in New York City alone.

Puerto Rico is predominantly Roman Catholic. Because the Roman Catholic Church forbids the use of birth control pills, there has traditionally been a strong opposition to birth control programs. The Family Planning Center was established in 1948, but it was not until the late 1960s that it gave free contraceptives to women on the island. When Luis Ferré became the governor of Puerto Rico in 1968, he made contraceptives and information on birth control available on a widespread basis in government centers.

Puerto Rico has one of the highest standards of living in Latin America, but it is far behind even the poorest states in the United States. The average yearly income per person in Puerto Rico is $10,000.

Go to vgsbooks.com for information about ethnic groups in Puerto Rico. You'll also find links to websites with up-to-date population figures and other statistics.

Health

Puerto Rico has one of the best health care systems in the Caribbean. An average of one doctor exists for every 387 people on the island. There are sixty-three hospitals, including eight public and fifty-five private hospitals.

After it became a commonwealth, the island's health care and sanitation improved greatly. In the 1950s, the government took over the operation of most of Puerto Rico's health care system. The Department of Health became responsible for the funding of Puerto Rico's seven medical regions and community health centers. When Pedro Rosselló became the governor in 1992, he advocated selling some of the government-run health care facilities to private owners. The proceeds were used to establish a medical plan for poor people.

The current health reform model stresses a preventive approach, such as educating people about healthy lifestyles. A government insurance plan is in place, with financial status determining cost. As a result, poor people pay less than those who have more money.

Puerto Rico's rate of infant mortality is 10.5 infant deaths per 1,000 live births. The average Puerto Rican can expect to live to the age of 75 years. The leading cause of death in Puerto Rico

Thanks to a strong health care system, Puerto Rican **infants and adults** can both expect to live long lives.

is heart disease, followed by malig-
nant tumors (cancer), and diabetes.

AIDS

AIDS is the fourth leading
cause of death in the general
population of Puerto Rico.
However, it is the leading cause
of death in men and women
between the ages of 25 and 49.
The rate of AIDS cases is high in
Puerto Rico. For every 100,000
people, there are 37 with AIDS, and 63
percent of the Puerto Ricans who contract
AIDS die of the disease each year.

A program called
Pro Familia was
established in Puerto Rico
in 1954 and continues to this
day. In the late 1960s, it
dispensed free contraceptives to
women on the island. It has
centers in thirteen municipalities.
Pro Familia provides workshops
on how to avoid AIDS and
also sells contraceptives
at a discount.

The main risk factors for contracting the disease are needle sharing
among male drug users and heterosexual relations with an infected
partner in women. Free government-run HIV/AIDS clinics are located
around the island. The government has also instituted programs to
raise people's awareness of AIDS prevention.

Due to a large number of cases in Puerto Rico, **AIDS education groups** are
active and widespread.

Literacy is stressed by the Puerto Rican educational system. Nine out of ten Puerto Ricans over the age of 15 can read and write.

Education

Puerto Rico has an excellent educational system, and the island boasts a very high literacy rate. In 1898 only about 23 percent of island inhabitants could read and write. At that time, education was mainly an option for the upper classes. But a century later, more than 90 percent of the adult population was literate.

In 2002 there were 1,537 public schools and 576 private schools on the island. During the 2001–2002 academic year, 604,093 students attended the island's public schools. At the same time, 140,443 students went to Puerto Rico's private schools. Nearly half of the island's employed residents have completed 13 or more years of education.

Puerto Rico's early formal schooling started with the Spanish colonists. Under Spanish rule, when the sons of Taíno chiefs reached the age of thirteen, they were required to live with Catholic missionaries for four years to learn the Catholic religion, reading, and writing. During the 1500s and 1600s, education on the island was compulsory only for males between the ages of six and twelve. Eventually, the schools were under the authority of the island's governor.

When the United States took over Puerto Rico in 1898, management of the island's school system was brought under the direction of an American commissioner of education. In 1899 education was made compulsory. The island's public schools adopted a system similar to that of the United States. All schools in Puerto Rico were then required to teach classes in English. However, in 1949 this policy was reversed. Since then, Spanish continues to be the language of instruction in the island's schools, but English is also taught as a compulsory second language.

Since 1949 the island's governor has selected the secretary of education, who manages the Department of Education. At first, this department only had the authority to create policies for the island's public schools. In 1958 the Puerto Rican government expanded the department's authority to include private schools.

As a result of these efforts, the island's residents are among the most educated in the entire Caribbean. Because the island's economy is based on manufacturing and service industries such as tourism, there is a strong need for an educated workforce. Puerto Rico has thirty-seven universities and colleges, and many islanders take advantage of the opportunity to obtain a higher education. In the 2001–2002 academic year, nearly two hundred thousand students enrolled in the island's universities.

The University of Puerto Rico, founded in 1903, is the oldest and largest public university on the island. It includes a school of medicine, a law school, a school of dentistry, and training for many other

A group of girls from a private school pose for the camera on a San Juan street. Private schools are partially managed by the Department of Education.

A **San Juan college student** reads notices on a campus bulletin board. San Juan is home to more than thirty colleges and universities.

advanced careers. The University of Puerto Rico features eleven campuses, including those in San Juan, Rio Piedras, and Ponce. Tuition at the university has been kept at a low cost due to heavy government subsidies (government donations of money).

The Inter-American University of Puerto Rico is the island's largest privately owned university. It has campuses in San Germán and nine other cities including San Juan, Arecibo, and Hato Rey. The four campuses of the Catholic University of Puerto Rico are located in Arecibo, Guayama, Ponce, and Mayagüez.

The University of Puerto Rico includes botanical gardens in Rio Piedras. The gardens showcase more than two hundred varieties of tropical and subtropical vegetation, including an orchid garden with tens of thousands of colorful, exotic flowers.

CULTURAL LIFE

Puerto Rico has a rich cultural heritage that evolved from the lifeways of the Taíno Indians, the Spaniards, and the Africans. The U.S. takeover also left its mark on the island. Together these diverse influences have created a vibrant culture that is uniquely Puerto Rican.

▶ Languages

When the Spaniards colonized Puerto Rico, they brought their language with them. In 1898 U.S. officials made English the compulsory language of instruction in all of Puerto Rico's schools. Unfortunately, many of the teachers did not speak English themselves.

In 1948 Luis Muñoz Marín, the first popularly elected governor of Puerto Rico, again made Spanish the language of instruction in schools on all levels, but English was taught as a second language. Eventually, in 1993 both English and Spanish were declared the two official languages of Puerto Rico. But Spanish remains the predominant language of the island.

Puerto Rican Spanish is flavored with some unique local pronunciations. Some words have also entered the island's vocabulary from the Taíno, African, and English languages.

Literature

Puerto Rico has had many fine poets. One of the most well-known was Eugenio María de Hostos. Born in Mayagüez in 1839, he was also a sociologist, an educator, and a revolutionary. Manuel Alonso, who was born in San Juan in 1823, was a doctor as well as a writer. In 1849 he wrote *El Gíbaro*, a collection of poetry that is considered the first Puerto Rican literary classic. In his book, Alonso describes, among other events, a jíbaro wedding, dances, and Christmas festivities. Alonso modeled his verse after the speech patterns of the jíbaros of the time.

Lola Rodríguez de Tío, born in 1843, is one of Puerto Rico's most esteemed nineteenth-century poets. She wrote the original lyrics to

Do You Speak "Spanglish"?

"Spanglish" is a mixture of Spanish and English. Some Puerto Ricans, especially those who have lived in both the United States and on the island, may speak Spanish, but they pepper their speech with words taken directly from English. They might talk about *jonrones* (home runs) at a *béisbol* (baseball) game. They may also speak part of a sentence in Spanish and the rest in English. Many educated people on the island disapprove of this use of added English words, because they feel it takes away from the purity of the Spanish language.

"La Borinqueña," the island's national anthem. Rodríguez de Tío was a staunch advocate of independence for Puerto Rico. She was also an early feminist who wrote essays on women's issues.

Another acclaimed nineteenth-century poet was José Gautier Benítez. Both his mother and his maternal aunt were accomplished poets, and he was surrounded by their literary influences as he grew up. His poetry deals with emotions and romantic love. Virgilio Dávila was born in 1869 and became part of the literary movement known as *criollismo.* This poetic movement praised the culture and landscapes of Puerto Rico.

Twentieth-century literary figures from the island include Enrique Laguerre, Julia de Burgos, and René Marqués. Laguerre became the most renowned novelist of the 1900s. Laguerre's books tackled the island's political and social problems. Manuel Zeno Gandía also wrote about political themes.

Later Puerto Rican writers of the twentieth century include Pedro Juan Soto and José Luis González. Soto's novels, short stories, and plays are fiction, revolving around the themes of Puerto Ricans in New York City. José Luis González also concerned himself with the literary theme of cultural identity in Puerto Rico.

Music

The earliest rhythms of Puerto Rico were those of the native Taínos who fashioned instruments out of tree trunks or gourds. They filled these objects with beans or stones and shook them to make a noise. These drums and maracas are still used in modern Latin music. The güiro, which is another native instrument, is played by running a metallic fork against a notched gourd.

After the Spaniards colonized the island, Puerto Ricans created variations on the guitar. The

Güiro

A ten-stringed small-bodied guitar called the **cuatro** *(the four instruments in the background)* is Puerto Rico's national instrument.

cuatro, the national instrument of Puerto Rico, is somewhat smaller than a standard guitar and has five pairs of strings.

Beginning in the nineteenth century, the *danza,* an elegant and romantic style of partner dancing, became popular in Puerto Rico. "La Borinqueña" was a danza before it was rearranged and set to the rhythms of a patriotic song.

Traditional Puerto Rican musical forms that are still performed at modern festivals are *bomba* and *plena.* Bomba music, which features wooden drums and maracas, has strong African roots and evolved from the rhythms created by slaves brought to the island. Plena is a music and dance form that uses percussion instruments such as conga drums and tambourines.

Perhaps the most widely popular contemporary Puerto Rican music is salsa. This lively type of music emerged in the second half of the twentieth century and continues to be extremely popular all over the world. The origins of the style are generally attributed to the late Tito Puente, a musician who was born to Puerto Rican parents in New York City's Spanish Harlem, and other Cuban musicians who also lived there.

Salsa music is characterized by a quick tempo and an Afro-Caribbean style. The musicians play bongo drums, conga drums,

A couple moves to the music during a Christmas celebration. Music and **dancing** are important parts of Puerto Rican culture and national identity.

guïros, maracas, cowbells, and other percussion instruments to create the catchy rhythms that invite people to dance. Noted salsa singers include Gilberto Santa Rosa, Willie Colón, Isabel Chacón, and the late Hector Lavoe.

Younger audiences enjoy the music of Menudo, an all-boy pop group. Latin pop music coming from Puerto Rico features singers Ricky Martin (formerly of Menudo) and New York City-born Marc Anthony and Jennifer Lopez.

Classical music is also popular in Puerto Rico. Pablo Casals, the famous cellist, was born in 1876 in Spain to a Puerto Rican mother and a Spanish father. In 1956 he moved to Puerto Rico, where he founded the Puerto Rico Symphony Orchestra and the Puerto Rico Music Conservatory. He also created the Casals Music Festival, which draws classical musicians from all over the world to Puerto Rico to perform for ten days in early June each year.

If you'd like to learn more about Puerto Rican culture, visit vgsbooks.com where you'll find links to recipes, photographs, basic Spanish words, and more.

Art

Some of the earliest known art in Puerto Rico is Taíno. Taíno artists used wood and stone to fashion small idols called *cemis*. They also made gold jewelry and ceramics. Since the colonial era, folk artists have crafted *santos*, wooden statues of the saints, which are often painted and decorated with metal or precious stones. Originally carved by religious Catholics, santos have also become prized for their artistic value.

The first Puerto Rican artist who painted in the European tradition was José Campeche. Born in 1751 in San Juan, he was the son of a freed slave. Campeche's first art teacher was his father, and then he went on to study painting with noted island artists. He created hundreds of paintings ranging from religious art to portraits, but few have survived.

Nineteenth-century artist Francisco Oller de Cestero (1833–1917) left Puerto Rico to study in Spain and France. He was influenced by acclaimed French painters like Gustave Courbet, Edouard Manet, Camille Pissarro, and Paul Cezanne. His work spans many subjects including stunning portrayals of the Puerto Rican landscape. His best-known work is *El Velorio*, a painting that depicts a traditional wake held for an infant.

During the early part of the twentieth century, artists such as Miguel Pou and Ramon Frade became known. After World War II (1939–1945), Lorenzo Homar and Rafael Tufiño were among the most popular artists. In the 1940s, political posters became popular, and Puerto Rican artists created woodcuts, linoleum blocks, and silk screen poster art. In the latter part of the twentieth century, most Puerto Rican artists learned their techniques in other countries. Among the acclaimed contemporary artists are Rafael Ferrer, Myrna Baez, and Jorge Zeno.

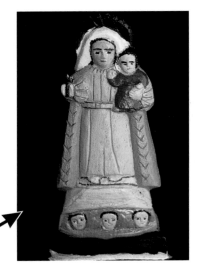

A brightly colored **santo** of Mary and the baby Jesus

Puerto Rico has numerous art galleries and museums. Among the most famous is the Ponce Museum of Art. The building was designed by Edward Durrell Stone, the architect who designed the Museum of Modern Art in New York City. The immense art collection in Ponce is one of the best in the Caribbean, including paintings by international artists such as Jan van Eyck, Auguste Rodin, and Peter Paul Rubens.

The latest art museum on the island is the Puerto Rico Museum of Art in Santurce. The museum opened its doors in June 2000. Its holdings include the most extensive collection of Puerto Rican art in the world, as well as many examples of the works of international artists.

Architecture

Puerto Rico's architectural styles run the gamut from early Spanish colonial to ultramodern. In Old San Juan, some pastel-colored Spanish houses have been standing since the early settlement of the city. Ornate churches that date from Spanish colonial times are also found in this area.

San Juan features modern buildings and shopping malls much like those in the United States. New and renovated hotels line the beaches in the Condado and Isla Verde sections of San Juan. Modern

Pastel-colored apartment buildings brighten the streets of Old San Juan.

architecture is found in Hato Rey, San Juan's financial center, which is filled with high-rise buildings framed in glass and steel.

Sports and Recreation

Puerto Ricans are avid fans of a variety of sports, including horseracing and cockfighting. One of the most popular sports in Puerto Rico is béisbol, or baseball, a game that was imported from the United States. Because of the island's sunny, warm climate, baseball can be played almost every day of the year. The island has produced a number of famous players including Hiram Bithorn—the first Puerto Rican to play in the American major leagues—Roberto Clemente, and Orlando Cepeda.

Baseball was considered the national sport of Puerto Rico, but more recently, basketball has taken the top spot. The sport's popularity grew quickly in the 1970s. Two of the island's best-known basketball stars include Pachín Vicens and Rúben Rodríguez. Each player has a sports arena on the island named after him.

Additional sports on the island include golf, tennis, and surfing. Puerto Rican tennis stars include Charlie Pasarell and Gigi Fernández. Puerto Rican golf celebrity Juan "Chi Chi" Rodríguez has won nearly forty professional golf tournaments.

Other famous Puerto Rican athletes include Jose "Chegui" Torres, a boxing champion in the

"RIFLE ARM" CLEMENTE

The most famous Puerto Rican baseball player was Roberto Clemente, sometimes called "Rifle Arm" Clemente. He was born into a poor family in Carolina in 1934. His immense talent for baseball became apparent when he was 18, and the Brooklyn Dodgers signed him on. Then in 1955, Clemente joined the Pittsburgh Pirates as an outfielder. He was actively involved in social causes on the island and beyond. Tragically, he died in an airplane crash in 1972 while en route to deliver medical supplies to the victims of an earthquake in Nicaragua. Clemente was inducted into the Baseball Hall of Fame shortly after his death.

1960s, and Félix "Tito" Rodriguez, who became the World Boxing Association's middleweight champion in 2001.

⊙ Food

Taíno, African, and Spanish influences have been blended to create a unique, delicious Puerto Rican cuisine. Before the Spaniards arrived, the Taínos ate native foods, such as yams, cassava, fruit, and meat from iguanas, guinea pigs, turtles, and other animals.

When the Spaniards colonized the island, they brought many of their own foods, including coffee, bananas, plantains, citrus fruits, garlic and other spices, cattle, goats, and pigs. Eventually, the native foods and the Spanish imports mixed to create a new type of cuisine.

Puerto Rican dishes include a tasty blend of rice dishes, such as *arroz con gandules*, or pigeon peas and rice; and *arroz con pollo* or chicken with rice cooked in coconut milk. Thick, hearty stews such

PIGEON PEAS AND RICE

Arroz con gandules is a tasty Puerto Rican dish made with rice, pigeon peas, and spices. Substitute small red kidney beans if pigeon peas aren't available. Serve with chicken or beef.

2 tbsp. oil

1 small onion, chopped

2 cloves garlic, crushed

4 tbsp. tomato paste

2 ripe tomatoes, chopped

1 green bell pepper, cored, seeded, and chopped

½ tsp. dried thyme

4 tbsp. fresh cilantro, chopped

1 16-oz can pigeon peas or red kidney beans, drained

1 c. long-grain white rice

2 c. water

2 tbsp. fresh lime juice

1. Heat the oil in a saucepan. Add the onion and fry gently for 5 minutes. Add the garlic, tomato paste, chopped ripe tomatoes, green peppers, and thyme and continue frying for 1 minute longer.
2. Add the cilantro, pigeon peas, and rice and fry, stirring frequently, for 1 minute.
3. Add the water and lime juice and cook gently, covered, for 15 minutes until the rice is tender. Add hot pepper sauce, salt, and freshly ground black pepper to taste, and serve.

Pineapples, bananas, plantains, coconuts, and other **fresh fruit** are a huge part of the traditional Puerto Rican diet.

as *asopao* are made from chicken, pork, or fish. Fried plantains, fritters (called *tostones*), and *sofrito* (a spicy sauce made with tomatoes, garlic, onions, chili peppers, and other seasonings) are commonly found on Puerto Rican dinner tables.

A popular island dessert is flan, a sweet egg custard. There are abundant fruits grown on the island, including guavas, pineapples, passionfruit, and papayas. At Christmastime, a traditional dessert is *arroz con dulce,* a type of rice pudding.

◉ Holidays and Festivals

Puerto Ricans celebrate holidays such as Christmas, New Year's Day, and the Fourth of July, but they also honor special days that aren't commonly celebrated in the United States. Some major holidays in Puerto Rico include Three Kings Day, Eugenio María de Hostos Day, Luis Muñoz Rivera's birthday, and Constitution Day. Puerto Rican children look forward to Three Kings Day, celebrated on January 6,

This trio of boys is decked out for **Three Kings Day.** Puerto Rican children love this early January holiday, as it brings post-Christmas gifts.

because they receive gifts said to come from the Three Wise Men. On January 8, Eugenio María de Hostos Day honors the life of this Puerto Rican political activist, sociologist, and poet. Puerto Ricans celebrate Luis Muñoz Rivera's birthday on July 17. Constitution Day, celebrated on July 25, commemorates the day in 1950 when Puerto Rico became a commonwealth and Puerto Ricans created their own constitution.

In addition to holidays, festivals are held throughout the island. In

Fiesta patronál

accordance with Catholic tradition, towns in Puerto Rico have their own patron saints, and lively celebrations called *fiestas patronales* (patron saint festivals) take place each year to pay homage to these saints. The festivals last about ten days and feature music, dancing, and festive foods. Among the offerings are *alcapuria*—fried plantains stuffed with a variety of fillings including different types of meat; *mavi*, a fizzy alcoholic drink made from plant bark; and traditional rice and beans served with meat. Each month of the year, there is at least one patron saint festival going on somewhere in Puerto Rico.

The feast of Saint John the Baptist, the patron saint of San Juan, takes place in late June. On June 23, thousands of people spend the night on the beach, which is brightly lit by bonfires. At the stroke of midnight, celebrants wade backward into the water to symbolize the baptism of Jesus. Tradition holds that the sea is blessed at this time, and walking into the water is said to bring good luck and good health in the coming year.

Every July the coastal town of Loíza holds its colorful Festival de Santiago Apóstal (Saint James the Apostle Festival). Most of the townspeople are of African descent, and this heritage is reflected in the lively bomba music featured at the festival. One highlight of the celebration is the appearance of *vejigantes,* people dressed in costumes made from multicolored scraps of material, sporting grotesque masks crowned by long, thin horns. These masked figures run through the crowds that assemble during the festival, playfully frightening people and dancing to the music.

This typical **vejigante** costume includes a papier-mâché mask and brightly colored robe of rags.

THE ECONOMY

Early on, Puerto Rico's economy was based on agriculture, and sugarcane was the dominant crop. This changed when the United States introduced a program called Operation Bootstrap in the 1940s. From that time until well into the 1980s, Puerto Rico developed a lucrative industrial economy based on manufacturing. Since the 1980s, however, Puerto Rico's economy has shifted its focus to service industries such as tourism.

Puerto Rico is the most industrialized island in the Caribbean, and its standard of living is one of the highest in the area. In 1999 Puerto Rico's gross domestic product (GDP) increased 4.2 percent after steadily growing at an average rate of 3.1 percent for the previous six years. (The gross domestic product is the total value of goods and services that are produced in one year in a region.)

Although Puerto Rico's per capita annual income is only $10,000, this is one of the highest in Latin America. The unemployment rate on the island was 10.5 percent in 2001, and the inflation rate was 4.8 percent.

Puerto Rico's economy continues to be closely tied to that of the United States. The island observes U.S. federal laws and regulations, so Puerto Ricans do not have to pay customs (import taxes) on products imported from the United States. The U.S. minimum wage also applies to Puerto Rican workers. Puerto Rico receives U.S. federal aid. The United States contributes more than $13 billion annually.

○ Operation Bootstrap

In the mid-1940s, Luis Muñoz Marín and others put together a plan to transform Puerto Rico's economy so it would not be completely dependent on agriculture. Muñoz Marín realized that having an economy dependent on just a few crops could be disastrous if bad weather conditions developed and the crops did not grow well. He saw an expansion of the manufacturing sector as the answer.

The industrial development of Operation Bootstrap began after World War II and continued until 1964. It stressed a Puerto Rican economy focused on manufacturing and tourism. Shortly after the plan was put into operation, more than twenty thousand jobs in the manufacturing sector became available.

In the 1950s, Puerto Rico actively campaigned to attract Americans to invest in factories in Puerto Rico. As a result, hundreds of new facilities were built on the island. The Ford Motor Company, for example, built a factory to manufacture car parts. These various U.S. companies spent close to $500 million on these factories, which manufactured clothing, medicine, machinery, and other products.

This economic progress slowed down in 1973, when oil prices rose steeply and a recession followed. At this time, some companies left the island and relocated to countries whose workers received lower minimum wages. Unemployment rose to nearly 20 percent of the island's workforce.

Then in 1976, Operation Bootstrap evolved into Section 936, a clause in the U.S. Internal Revenue Code, which gave considerable tax exemptions to American companies that invested in Puerto Rico. This brought many new factories to the island, including those that produced pharmaceuticals and chemicals. Electronics companies, such as Intel, which manufactures computer components, also flocked to the island. However, in 1985 some members of the U.S. Congress tried to abolish Section 936. Then-governor Rafael Hernández Colón suggested linking the section to President Ronald Reagan's Caribbean Basin Initiative (CBI), and Section 936 remained in force.

Some of the highest paid Puerto Rican workers in the manufacturing industries work for pharmaceutical firms.

The CBI program allowed companies to set up factories in various Caribbean islands where products would be partially completed by a workforce that was paid less than laborers in Puerto Rico. The final stages of production would be completed in Puerto Rico, and the tax benefits of Section 936 would apply. By 1989 the tax breaks has lured enough U.S. companies to generate 275,000 more jobs in Puerto Rico.

But in 1996, Section 936 was eliminated for new companies on the island. It will be phased out over a period of ten years for existing companies that profited from the tax exemptions in the past. By 2005 Section 936 will be completely eliminated.

Although Operation Bootstrap was responsible for the restructuring of Puerto Rico's economy and created many jobs, critics contend that many of the benefits of the rapid economic growth went to U.S.

corporations. After closing their factories, these companies took their profits back to the United States. Yet both advocates and critics of the program agree that Operation Bootstrap was instrumental in creating one of the most educated labor forces in the Caribbean and in Latin America.

Manufacturing

Because of the incentive provided by tax exemptions in the past, manufacturing remains a strong part of Puerto Rico's economy. Almost 40 percent of the island's production is in the manufacturing sector. More than 90 percent of the island's exports are manufactured. Puerto Rico makes pharmaceuticals, electronics, textiles, chemicals, electrical equipment, machinery, scientific instruments, and other products. Canned tuna is another big export.

Puerto Rico's leading trading partner is the United States. In 2001 Puerto Rican exports to the United States totaled more than $41 billion. Many of the pharmaceuticals bought in the United States come from

Employees at a Puerto Rican **chemical plant** wear masks and gloves for protection. Chemicals are one of Puerto Rico's top exports.

Puerto Rico. Imports from the United States to the island totaled more than $15 billion. Food, consumer items, chemicals, electrical equipment, and crude petroleum are among the products that are most often imported to the island. Puerto Rico also conducts a considerable amount of trade with other countries, including Japan, Ireland, Germany, Venezuela, and the United Kingdom. In the Caribbean, the Dominican Republic is one of Puerto Rico's greater trading partners.

San Juan, Ponce, and Mayagüez are the three main ports in Puerto Rico. All have free trade zones or foreign trade zones. These are places located near transportation centers, such as seaports, where importers can store, assemble, and exhibit their goods to avoid paying regular customs duties. For example, if a nation ships a food product like orange juice in bulk to a foreign trade zone and then bottles it and labels it there, they will pay a lower customs duty. If the orange juice were already labeled and bottled when it arrived at the port, the importer would have to pay a higher duty, and the consumers would have to pay a higher price on the imported item.

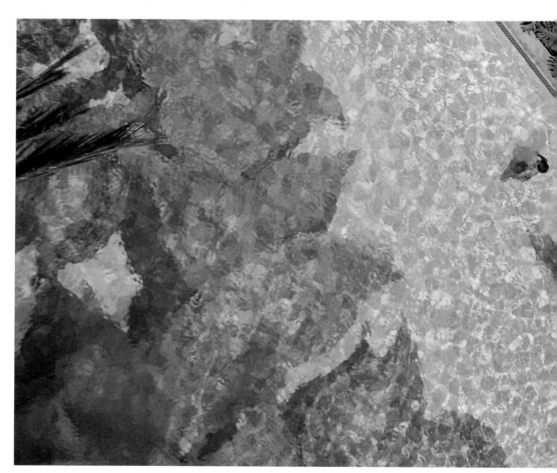

Service Industries

Service industries—such as tourism, banking, insurance, and real estate—provide services rather than goods. Taken together, Puerto Rico's service industries constitute the largest part of the island's GDP.

The Puerto Rican government is encouraging the expansion of the tourism industry. With the island's warm climate and beautiful beaches, tourism is rapidly becoming a growing source of income. Puerto Rico has full-scale destination resorts. These larger hotels provide accommodations plus on-site restaurants and recreation such as tennis and golf. Other visitors take advantage of fine hotels, cozy inns, and rented condos. In 2001, 2.6 million hotel rooms were rented, which amounted to an occupancy rate of 67 percent. Tourists to Puerto Rico spent more than $2.5 million during 2000 and 2001. This was an increase of about 6 percent over the 1999 to 2000 period. About three million visitors, mostly Americans, travel to the island every year.

Old San Juan's El Convento hotel, built more than three hundred years ago, was originally a convent for Carmelite nuns.

Tourists relax at one of Puerto Rico's many resort hotels. Tourism is the backbone of the Puerto Rican economy.

Puerto Rico is a major Caribbean seaport. Huge ocean liners transport millions of tons of cargo to and from the island each year.

Transportation

Luis Muñoz Marín International Airport, located east of downtown San Juan in Isla Verde, accommodated 10 million passengers in 2001. In the same year, Puerto Rico transported more than 258,500 tons (234,507 metric tons) of air cargo and 9,600,000 tons (more than 8,709,120 metric tons) of ocean cargo. Ocean transport accounts for most of the island's international commerce.

The island has never had a railway system. However, the government is spending $1.6 billion on San Juan's elevated train network, which will be opening in phases in the near future. The first phase will connect Bayamón, Guaynabo, and Santurce. Another phase will link Rio Piedras to Carolina's municipality. A third phase will connect San Juan to Luis Muñoz Marín International Airport.

Puerto Rico has an extensive system of paved roads. The island's transportation network includes 4,604 miles (7,409 km) of roads, 160 miles (258.5 km) of highways, and 114 miles (183.8 km) of expressways.

Agriculture and Fishing

Puerto Rico went from a farming economy to a manufacturing economy. But farmers cultivate many tropical fruits, including bananas, plantains, pineapples, coconuts, papayas, guavas, mangoes, citrus fruits, and breadfruit. Pumpkins and tomatoes also grow on Puerto Rico. Sugarcane is no

Although sugarcane is no longer Puerto Rico's primary crop, it is still important to the economy. **Sugarcane farms** like this one provide raw materials for producing rum, granulated sugar, and molasses.

longer the dominant crop, but farmers still grow it. Factories process the stalks into molasses, white sugar, and rum. Coffee is also an important crop on the island.

Farmers raise beef cattle, pigs, and poultry for meat, and they also keep chickens for eggs. About half the farms are family run, and the other farms belong to Puerto Rican-owned corporations. Deep-sea fishing is another industry that contributes to the island's economy. In the deep waters surrounding the island, fishing crews reel in tuna, grouper, mahimahi, sardines, bass, and red snapper.

⊙ Mining, Forestry, and Construction

Puerto Rico's leading mined products are stone, lime, sand, and gravel. Cement is also produced on the island. Another natural resource of

FROM SUGARCANE TO ALCOHOL

One outgrowth of the sugarcane industry was the production of rum. When molasses, a sugarcane by-product, is mixed with yeast, it begins to ferment and produces an alcoholic drink. When this liquid is refined, the final product is called rum.

The Bacardi Rum plant in Puerto Rico is one of the largest in the world. It can produce 100,000 gallons (378,500 liters) of rum per day and 221 million cases of the beverage annually. Visitors can tour the Bacardi facilities, which include a museum called the Cathedral of Rum.

Puerto Rico's rain forests are a source of natural beauty and ecological importance.

the island is its forests. In 1995, 31 percent of the total land area of Puerto Rico was covered by preserved forests.

Visit vgsbooks.com where you will find links to up-to-date information about Puerto Rico's economy.

The Future

Despite some problems, such as overpopulation, Puerto Ricans look forward to a bright future. With the continued expansion of its service industries and manufacturing, the island may one day see a time when it will no longer depend on U.S. federal funds. A project called the Golden Triangle is a huge proposed development slated to be completed in 2005 that will extend from Condado to Old San Juan. It will encompass world trade centers and a new convention center, malls, museums, parks, and other attractions. Puerto Ricans view this development as an efficient way to give the island a new, more global economy.

Less certain is the future of Puerto Rico's status. Will Puerto Rico remain a commonwealth, gain its independence, or become the next state? Only time will tell. But whatever the island's status, one thing is certain—the people of the island, with their warmth and close family ties, their rich heritage, and their vibrant culture, will continue to gain strength from their national identity and to approach the future with high expectations, ambition, and purpose.

If Puerto Rico ever attained U.S. statehood, it would be the poorest of the states, according to residents' incomes.

A group of flags, including **the Puerto Rican flag (center),** the American flag (top), and a military flag, fly high above El Morro.

CA. A.D. 100 The Archaic Indians inhabit what would become Puerto Rico.

CA. A.D. 700 The Indians of the Igneri culture inhabit what would become Puerto Rico.

CA. 1000 The Taíno Indians establish a civilization on the island.

1493 Christopher Columbus and his crew arrive. Columbus calls the island San Juan Bautista (Saint John the Baptist).

1508 Juan Ponce de León establishes Puerto Rico's first settlement at Caparra.

1510 Spain appoints Juan Ponce de León as governor of San Juan Bautista (Puerto Rico).

1511 The island of San Juan Bautista (Puerto Rico) is given a coat of arms. It is the first Spanish colony in the New World to have one. The Taínos revolt against the Spaniards, but the rebellion is put down by Ponce de León.

1521 The name of the island is changed to Puerto Rico.

1539 The Spaniards begin the construction of San Felipe del Morro (El Morro) fort on the western tip of Old San Juan.

1595 The British try to take over the island but are repelled.

1625 The Dutch attack the island but later retreat.

1630 The Spaniards begin to construct seven fortresses connected by stone walls and three gates to protect the entire city of San Juan.

1702 The British attack the island once more and are again unsuccessful.

1797 The British attack the island a third time. This was the last foreign attack on Puerto Rico.

1868 El Grito de Lares uprising takes place. Revolutionaries seeking independence from Spain march into the town of Lares, but the rebellion is put down. This marks the beginning of the independence movement in Puerto Rico.

1873 The Spanish government abolishes slavery on Puerto Rico.

1897 Spain issues the Autonomic Charter, and Puerto Rico is granted some local rule.

1898 The Spanish-American War breaks out on April 25. U.S. troops invade Puerto Rico on July 25. The United States wins the war in August. When the Treaty of Paris is signed on December 10, Spain surrenders its possessions of Puerto Rico, Guam, and the Philippines to the United States.

1900   The United States passes the Foraker Act. President McKinley appoints a governor to Puerto Rico. The act establishes that Puerto Rico belongs to the United States but that it is not a state.

1917   The United States passes the Jones Act, which grants American citizenship to Puerto Ricans.

1946   President Truman appoints Jesús Piñero as the first Puerto Rican-born governor of the island.

1948   Luis Muñoz Marín becomes the first popularly elected governor of Puerto Rico.

1949   Luis Muñoz Marín declares Spanish will be taught in all Puerto Rican schools, with English as a second language.

1950   On July 3, the U.S. Congress approves Public Law 600, which allows Puerto Ricans the right to create their own constitution. A Puerto Rican convention writes the constitution, which is similar to the U.S. Constitution. On November 1, Puerto Rican nationalists attempt to assassinate President Truman but fail.

1952   On July 25, the U.S. Congress declares Puerto Rico a U.S. commonwealth.

1954   Puerto Rican nationalists enter the U.S. House of Representatives and open fire. Five congressmen are wounded, and the four nationalists are sent to federal prisons.

1957   Cellist Pablo Casals establishes the Casals Festival.

1967   A plebiscite is held on the status of Puerto Rico. The majority of Puerto Ricans vote in favor of continued commonwealth status.

1981   The first cases of AIDS are reported in Puerto Rico.

1990   Antonia Coello de Novello becomes the first woman and the first Puerto Rican to be appointed as the U.S. surgeon general.

1993   Spanish and English are declared the two official languages of Puerto Rico. Another plebiscite is held. Once again the majority of voters favor commonwealth status.

1998   Hurricane Georges batters Puerto Rico, causing millions of dollars' worth of damage. A third plebiscite is held. More than 50 percent of the voters choose "none of the above." Forty-six percent vote for statehood.

1999   David Sanes Rodríguez, a civilian guard on Vieques, is accidentally killed by a stray U.S. Navy bomb on April 19. Protesters enter restricted navy areas and demand an end to bombing exercises.

2000   On May 4, federal authorities start arresting the Vieques protesters for trespassing on navy property.

2001   In January 2001, Sila Calderón, the first female governor of Puerto Rico, is sworn into office.

2003   On May 1, the U.S. Navy withdraws from Vieques.

COUNTRY NAME Commonwealth of Puerto Rico

AREA 3,435 square miles (8,896 sq. km)

MAIN LANDFORMS Cerro de Punta, Cordillera Central, Luquillo Mountains, Sierra de Cayey, El Yunque, Coastal Lowlands, Coastal Valleys

HIGHEST POINT Cerro de Punta, 4,389 feet (1,337 m) above sea level

LOWEST POINT Sea level

MAJOR RIVERS Arecibo River, La Plata River, Culebrinas River

ANIMALS Puerto Rican parrot, reinita, bats, iguanas, nonpoisonous snakes, guinea pigs, mongooses, coquí, blue parrot fish, leatherback sea turtles

CAPITAL CITY San Juan

OTHER MAJOR CITIES Bayamón, Carolina, Ponce, Caguas, Mayagüez

OFFICIAL LANGUAGE Spanish

MONETARY UNIT U.S. dollar. 100 cents = 1 dollar.

PUERTO RICAN CURRENCY

Because Puerto Rico is a U.S. possession, the currency used is the U.S. dollar. Bills come in denominations of 1, 5, 10, 20, 50, 100, and 1,000 dollars. Coins come in denominations of 1, 5, 10, 25, and 50 cents and 1 dollar.

The flag of Puerto Rico was created in 1895. It resembles the flag of Cuba, designed in 1849, because both islands had the common goal of seeking independence from Spain. The white star in the blue field represents Puerto Rico. This flag was officially adopted in 1952, when Puerto Rico became a commonwealth of the United States.

The official lyrics of "La Borinqueña" are by Manuel Fernández Juncos. (Earlier patriotic lyrics were written by Lola Rodríguez de Tío.) The original music was a danza by Félix Astol y Artés (although sometimes attributed to Francisco Ramírez), and Ramón Collado later gave the music the march arrangement of an anthem.

How beautiful Borinquén,
my peerless native land,
the verdant hills and valleys,
and palm encircled strand.

On thy fair bosom lovingly
the sun its radiance pours,
while murmuring waves with tenderness
caress thy sailing shore.

When thy rare beauty he first described,
with wonder thrilling, Columbus cried:
"Oh! Oh! Oh!"

No land like thee, Borinquén,
the world does know;
I shall meet with no other,
no other wherever I go.

For a link where you can listen to Puerto Rico's national anthem, "La Borinqueña," go to vgsbooks.com.

ROBERTO ALOMAR (b. 1968) Alomar is a baseball player from Ponce. Playing second base with the Toronto Blue Jays, he helped the team win the World Series in 1993. Winner of many Gold Glove Awards, Alomar began playing for the Cleveland Indians in 1999.

RAMÓN EMETERIO BETANCES (1827–1898) A physician and revolutionary, Betances wrote "The Ten Commandments of Free Men," the ideas that formed the roots of the Puerto Rican independence movement. Among his ten demands was the call for the abolition of slavery and the freedom of the people to elect their own governing officials. Betances was born in Cabo Rojo.

SILA CALDERÓN (b. 1942) Born in San Juan, Calderón was elected Puerto Rico's first female governor in 2000, after holding several government positions in the 1980s and 1990s.

JOSÉ CAMPECHE (1752–1809) One of the first acclaimed artists in the European tradition, Campeche was born in San Juan. He first learned how to paint from his father, a freed slave, and later studied with other painters. The subjects of his paintings vary from portraits to religious images.

ROBERTO CLEMENTE (1934–1972) One of the greatest baseball players in history, Clemente was born in Carolina. He played right field for the Pittsburgh Pirates, who won the World Series in 1960 and 1971 with Clemente's help. In 1972 he became the eleventh baseball player in major league history to get 3,000 hits.

ANTONIA COELLO DE NOVELLO (b. 1944) Fajardo-born Antonia Coello de Novello was the first woman and the first Hispanic American to serve as U.S. surgeon general (1991–1994). She aided in the development of the National Hispanic/Latino Health Initiative, a program for the improvement of health care for Hispanic Americans.

GIGI FERNÁNDEZ (b. 1964) Born in San Juan, Beatríz "Gigi" Fernández was the first professional female athlete in Puerto Rico and the first Puerto Rican to win two consecutive gold medals in the Olympics— in 1992 and 1996.

RAÚL JULIA (1940–1994) Born in Santurce, Julia later went to New York City and performed in the New York Shakespeare Festival. He eventually moved to Hollywood, where he starred in acclaimed movies like *The Addams Family* and *Kiss of the Spider Woman.*

JENNIFER LOPEZ (b. 1970) Born to Puerto Rican parents in the Bronx, New York, Lopez—also known as "J.Lo"—is one of the most famous Puerto Rican American entertainers. Known for her movie portrayal of the late singer Selena, Lopez has starred in numerous other movies

Famous People

including *The Wedding Planner, Enough,* and *Jersey Girl.* She also launched a highly successful singing career in 1999 with an album titled "On the Six." Subsequent albums "J.Lo" and "This is Me . . . Then" were also chart toppers.

RICKY MARTIN (b. 1971) Born in San Juan, Martin began acting in TV commercials at the age of six. He became a member of Menudo, an all-male pop group, and later joined the cast of the soap opera *General Hospital.* His 1999 single "Livin' La Vida Loca" made him an internationally known singer.

RITA MORENO (b. 1931) Born in Humacao, Moreno moved to New York as a child. She was the first performer to win all four of the highest entertainment awards—an Oscar (for the role of Anita in *West Side Story*), a Tony, an Emmy, and a Grammy.

LUIS MUÑOZ MARÍN (1898–1980) Considered one of the most important Puerto Rican politicians of the twentieth century, Muñoz Marín helped secure commonwealth status and also spearheaded Operation Bootstrap, an economic program that industrialized Puerto Rico. Muñoz Marín was born in San Juan.

LUIS MUÑOZ RIVERA (1859–1916) Barranquitas-born Rivera was a journalist and nationalist. He founded *La Democracia,* a newspaper later edited by his son Luis Muñoz Marín. He headed the first Puerto Rican cabinet under U.S. occupation, and pleaded for greater self-government. Faced with bitter political opposition in Puerto Rico, he moved to New York City. As resident commissioner of Puerto Rico in Washington, D.C., from 1910 to 1916, he campaigned for the United States to extend the rights of Puerto Ricans.

TITO PUENTE (1923–2000) Born in New York City's Spanish Harlem to Puerto Rican parents, Puente is known as the father of salsa music. A composer and arranger, he was also an accomplished pianist and saxophone player. He recorded more than one hundred albums. Carlos Santana's 1970s rendition of Puente's "Oye Como Va" became world famous.

FÉLIX "TITO" RODRIGUEZ (b. 1971) San Juan-born Rodriguez started boxing professionally at the age of seventeen. In May 2001, he defeated William Joppy to become the World Boxing Association's middleweight champion.

JUAN "CHI CHI" RODRIGUEZ (b. 1935) Born in Rio Piedras, Rodriguez became a golf caddie when he was only six years old. As an adult, he won eight professional golf championships and has had success on the senior golf tour. He later established the Chi Chi Rodriguez Foundation for troubled youth in Florida.

Sights to See

ARECIBO OBSERVATORY Nestled in northwestern Puerto Rico's karst country, the Arecibo Observatory is the world's largest radio telescope. Its immense dish covers 20 acres (8 hectares) and is suspended over a 563-foot (172-m) deep natural sinkhole. The dish can pick up the slightest sounds from faraway stars.

EL MORRO El Morro, Puerto Rico's most famous fortress, was designed to protect San Juan from attacks by foreign ships. Construction began on the site in 1539. The fort rises more than 140 feet (43 m) above the harbor, and some of its walls measure from 18 to 25 feet (5 to 8 m) thick.

EL YUNQUE The Caribbean National Forest is the only tropical rain forest within the U.S. National Forest system. With 28,000 acres (11,331 hectares), the forest contains well-maintained trails for visitors and features more than two hundred types of trees, fifty types of orchids, and other exotic plant life.

OLD SAN JUAN This older, traditional part of San Juan, located on the city's northwestern side, features cobblestone streets, museums, and colorful Spanish colonial houses adorned with wrought iron. Narrow, picturesque streets and plazas abound in this area.

RÍO CAMUY CAVE PARK This 268-acre (108-hectare) cave network is one of the largest in the world. Visitors take a tram down a mountain for a guided tour of Clara Cave, which features blind fish that are only found in this area.

THE TIBES INDIAN CEREMONIAL CENTER This center, north of Ponce, is one of the most important archaeological sites in Puerto Rico. It features ball courts, burial grounds, and plazas from a pre-Taíno culture dating from A.D. 300 to 700. There are also some reconstructed thatched huts and a small museum.

batey: the central plaza of a Taíno village

Boriquén: the Taíno name for Puerto Rico. It means "the land of the brave lord."

cacique: a Taíno chief

commonwealth: in the case of Puerto Rico, a self-governing possession of a nation. Puerto Rico is owned by the United States, and its residents are U.S. citizens who can vote in local elections.

coquí: a small tree frog that is found almost nowhere else but Puerto Rico. The coquí is known for its two-note song, "co-KEE," for which the frog is named.

free-trade zone (or foreign-trade zone): an area near a seaport or an airport where imported goods are stored, assembled, and exhibited. Countries that import their products to free-trade zones pay less than the regular customs duties on these products.

gross domestic product (GDP): the total value of goods and services that are produced in one year in a region

jíbaro: a rural worker. Most jíbaros were descendants of escaped Taínos who married and had children with Spanish deserters. They lived and worked in the mountainous countryside of Puerto Rico and are looked up to as folk heroes.

karst: a limestone region that contains caves and underground streams

mogote: the Spanish word for a haystack hill. These are structures found in the karst region, which is made of limestone.

nitaíno: a Taíno noble who functioned as an adviser to the chief

plebiscite: a vote on a specific issue. In Puerto Rico, there have been plebiscites to determine whether the people want their island to remain a commonwealth, to become a state, or to become independent from the United States.

santo: a carved, wooden statue of a saint. Folk artists create these statues and often paint and decorate them with metal or precious stones.

Census 2000 Data for Puerto Rico. October 31, 2002
Website: <www.census.gov/census2000/states/pr.html> (April 29, 2002)
This is a page on the official website of the U.S. Census Bureau. It contains information on the population of Puerto Rico, according to the results of the 2000 census. The information is broken down by places on the island.

Cruz Báez, Angel David, and Thomas D. Boswell. *Atlas of Puerto Rico.* **Miami, FL: The Cuban American National Council, Inc., 1997.**
This thorough book describes the geography of Puerto Rico and includes important facts about the people.

Fernandez, Ronald, et al. *Puerto Rico: Past and Present.* **Westport, CT: Greenwood Press, 1998.**
This book was written in the form of a mini-encyclopedia. It gives accurate, fairly recent information on Puerto Rico's history, politics, culture, and much more.

Fuson, Robert H. *Juan Ponce de León and the Spanish Discovery of Puerto Rico and Florida.* **Blacksburg, VA: The McDonald & Woodward Publishing Company, 2000.**
This book brims with information on the European discovery of Puerto Rico and Juan Ponce de León's time as governor.

Lombardi, Matt, ed. *Fodor's Puerto Rico.* **New York: Fodor's Travel Publications, 2001.**
This guidebook primarily describes places to stay on the island, but it also has information on the culture and lesser-known destinations. Three excerpts from articles and books on Puerto Rico provide a glimpse of some personal views of the island.

Morales Carrión, Arturo. *Puerto Rico: A Political and Cultural History.* **New York: W.W. Norton & Company, Inc., 1983.**
This is a book about Puerto Rico's history and culture by a distinguished historian who was an active politician and also the deputy assistant secretary of state for Latin America during the administration of John F. Kennedy.

Morris, Nancy. *Puerto Rico: Culture, Politics, and Identity.* **Westport, CT: Praeger Publishers, 1995.**
The author concerns herself with the cultural aspects of Puerto Rico. She interviewed many Puerto Ricans to find out how they view their own identity.

Perl, Lila. *Puerto Rico: Island Between Two Worlds.* **New York: William Morrow and Company, 1979.**
This book gives an overview of Puerto Rico's history from the era of its first inhabitants to more recent times.

Population Reference Bureau (January 1, 2002)
Website: <www.worldpop.org/datafinder.htm> (June 13, 2002)
This is the website of the Population Reference Bureau Data Sheet, which is updated annually. It contains statistics on different countries and their populations, birthrates, death rates, and other facts.

Selected Bibliography

Rouse, Irving. *The Taínos: Rise and Decline of the People Who Greeted Columbus.* **New Haven, CT: Yale University Press, 1992.**
This book includes facts about the native people who lived in Puerto Rico at the time of Columbus's voyage to the island.

The Stateman's Yearbook 2002: The Politics, Culture and Economics of the World. **New York: Palgrave, 2002.**
This book lists condensed facts such as social statistics, recent election results, and energy and natural resources in countries around the world.

Wagenheim, Kal, and Olga Jiménez de Wagenheim. *The Puerto Ricans: A Documentary History.* **Princeton, NJ: Markus Wiener Publishers, 1996.**
This book emphasizes Puerto Rico's modern history.

Altapedia Online
Website: <www.atlapedia.com>
This website offers full-color maps, key facts, and statistics on Puerto Rico and other countries of the world.

50states.com States and Capitals
Website: <www.50states.com>
This website has information on Puerto Rico and the United States.

Johnson, Rebecca L. *A Walk in the Rain Forest.* **Minneapolis: Carolrhoda Books, Inc., 2001.**
Explore the plant and animal life found in North America's rain forests, including those of Puerto Rico. For younger readers.

Johnston, Joyce. *Puerto Rico.* **Minneapolis: Lerner Publications Company, 2002.**
A book for younger readers, this volume provides basic information about Puerto Rico's land, history, people, economy, and environmental issues.

Kaufman, Cheryl Davidson. *Cooking the Caribbean Way.* **Minneapolis: Lerner Publications Company, 2002.**
This cultural cookbook provides recipes from all of the islands in the Caribbean, including a recipe for asopao from Puerto Rico.

Le Blanc, Beverley, ed. *The Complete Caribbean Cookbook.* **Edison, NJ: Chartwell Books, 1996.**
This collection of recipes features appetizers, main courses, and desserts from Puerto Rico and other Caribbean islands.

Levy, Patricia. *Puerto Rico.* **New York: Marshall Cavendish Corporation, 1997.**
This well-researched book provides an overview of Puerto Rico's people and culture.

Márquez, Herón. *Latin Sensations.* **Minneapolis: Lerner Publications Company, 2001.**
Follow the careers of Puerto Rican musicians Ricky Martin and Jennifer Lopez, among others, as they rocket to superstardom.

Muckley, Robert L., and Adela Martínez-Santiago. *Stories from Puerto Rico/Historias de Puerto Rico.* **Chicago: Passport Books, 1999.**
This book features English on one side of the book and its Spanish translation on facing pages. Readers can learn Spanish while reading tales of the Taínos, Puerto Rican legends, and stories about famous people from the island.

Ochoa, George. *The New York Public Library Amazing Hispanic American History: A Book of Answers for Kids.* **New York: John Wiley and Sons, 1998.**
This book gives the reader facts and solid information about Puerto Rico and other places with Hispanic populations that have moved to the United States.

Further Reading and Websites

Puerto Rico Herald
Website: <www.puertorico-herald.org>
This on-line newspaper in English and Spanish gives the latest news about Puerto Rico.

Puerto Rico Online Magazine
Website: <www.prmag.com>
This on-line magazine covers travel in Puerto Rico.

Puerto Rico Tourism Company/Travel Guide to Puerto Rico
Website: <www.gotopuertorico.com>
The official website of the Puerto Rico Tourism Company contains a wealth of information on places to see on the island, as well as a calendar of events and the daily temperature.

Puerto Rico WOW!
Website <www.puertoricoWOW.com>
This website has up-to-date, accurate information on Puerto Rico's demographics, politics, education, culture, and even the current social scene.

Temko, Florence. *Traditional Crafts from the Caribbean.* Minneapolis: Lerner Publications Company, 2001.
Learn to make vejigante costumes for the Festival de Santiago Apóstal and other fun items using a variety of everyday materials.

Unterberger, Amy L., ed. *Who's Who Among Hispanic Americans.* Detroit: Gale Research, Inc., 1992.
If you're looking for quick information about the lives of famous Puerto Ricans and other Hispanic Americans, this is the place to find it.

vgsbooks.com
Website: <http://www.vgsbooks.com>
Visit vgsbooks.com, the homepage of the Visual Geography Series®, which is updated regularly. You can get linked to all sorts of useful on-line information, including geographical, historical, demographic, cultural, and economic websites. The vgsbooks.com site is a great resource for late-breaking news and statistics.

Captions for photos appearing on cover and chapter openers:

Cover: An aging building in Old San Juan, part of Puerto Rico's bustling capital, overlooks the calm Caribbean.

pp. 4–5 Tamarindo Beach glows in the late morning light. Puerto Rico's stunning beaches attract about three million tourists every year.

pp. 8–9 Varied terrain and plant life characterize the lush environment of the island. This cactus and shrub-covered hill overlooks an islet that is part of the Culebra National Wildlife Refuge.

pp. 20–21 A dramatic illustration shows Christopher Columbus coming ashore in Puerto Rico, accompanied by soldiers, Christian missionaries, and noblemen.

pp. 36–37 Puerto Ricans crowd a float in a Christmas parade that winds through Old San Juan.

pp. 44–45 Street musicians play traditional Puerto Rican cuatro guitars as they roam the streets of San Juan.

pp. 56–57 This photo shows a collection of U.S. dollars and coins. Since Puerto Rico is a U.S. territory, the island uses American currency.

Photo Acknowledgments
The images in this book are used with the permission of: © Robert Fried, pp. 4–5, 8–9, 10, 15 (top), 16–17, 18, 41, 50, 60–61, 62, 64; Presentationmaps.com, pp. 6, 11; © Tony Arruza/CORBIS, p. 12; © Marc Bacon/Latin Focus.com, pp. 13, 59; © Suzanne Murphy-Larronde, pp. 14, 22 (top), 36–37, 39, 40, 42, 44–45, 46, 47, 48, 49, 53, 54 (both), 55, 63, 65; © Kevin Schafer/CORBIS, p.15 (bottom); © TRIP/J. Highet, p. 19; Library of Congress, pp. 20–21, 26; © Independent Picture Service, pp. 22 (bottom), 30; Puerto Rico General Archives, p. 24; Brown Brothers, pp. 25, 27; © CORBIS, p. 28; Commonwealth of Puerto Rico, Department of State, p. 29; © Bettmann/CORBIS, pp. 31, 51; © AFP/CORBIS, p. 33; © TRIP/D. Oliver, p. 35; © Kit Kittle/CORBIS, p. 38; © TRIP/J. Greenberg, p. 43; © Todd Strand/Independent Picture Service, pp. 56–57, 68.

Cover: © Suzanne Murphy-Larronde